Faces
of
Prayer

by Christopher Cross

Publishers · GROSSET & DUNLAP · New York
A FILMWAYS COMPANY

Also by Christopher Cross

Soldiers of God
My Fighting Congregation
Minute of Prayer For A World At War
Minute Of Prayer For All Occasions

Photo Credits

Eve Arnold   *Danny Lyon*
Henri Cartier-Bresson *Roger Malloch*
Bruce Davidson   *Costa Manos*
Elliott Erwitt   *Mary E. Mark*
Leonard Freed   *McKiernan*
Paul Fusco   *Wayne Miller*
Philip Jones Griffiths *Maurice Rosen*
Burt Glinn   *Dennis Stock*
Charles Harbutt

*The author is grateful to H. Robert Armstrong
and to the staff of Magnum for their cooperation.*

Faces of Prayer

Of all
that
God makes...

And pain
turned to
joy

Now, we're
blessed by
You

I'm not
alone,
Lord

God,
do You
love us...

Is it lonely
up there
God?

Do animal's
prayers get
heard too?

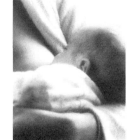
Give him
Your
sustenance...

Help him
to connect
Oh, Lord

Jesus, hear
my song

Faces
of
Prayer

What is your language, God?
How shall I speak to You?
Do You hear me when I cry?
Do You see me when I'm sad?
How do You know when I need You?
And the child asks the questions
only the innocent can ask:
Does God understand my language?
How can He listen and understand
when so many are praying?

At sundown and at sunup; at appointed holy days; in times of personal need we raise our voices to our God...Saviour...Jehovah... Supreme Being...Buddha...Allah.

Or we close our eyes, raise our voices; make our supplications to that mystic power that is sometimes nameless...a benevolent power whose revelations may be felt in the trunk of a tree as it moves imperceptably out of the ground into space to reveal the miracle of life; sunlight caressing, dancing on leaves now green, soon golden.

Wherever, however, whoever we are - we make our chants, sing our songs, speak our words of thanks, of regrets, of hope and of joy.

But there is still another kind of praying. It goes on all the time as we work and play; as we love and wonder; as we strive and suffer; as we live and die.

And we can see it, feel it all around us.

It's in the faces of children as they suffer the pain of an injured pet; as they gaze with awe at the sky above, at the sea rolling in, at the blinking eyes of a frog.

There are meaningful discoveries in the faces of the old as they search for those who have died; as they embrace the young in their lives.

There are beauty and wisdom, wonder and hope to perceive in the faces of parents as they look at the miracle of their newborn; as they gaze with anxiety into a future that seems uncertain.

In the faces of the deprived, the outcast, the frightened, there are to be found their prayers to be made a part of the good earth.

Then, too, there are the prayers of thanksgiving in the faces of those who have found the meaning of life, of love, of sharing and caring.

It is prayer that does not come from the throat, alone.

It is the prayer that is quiet...but eloquent. It is the prayer that flows, most often unnoticed, from deep within to express our most private, yet universal, anxieties and aspirations.

The faces of those around us can tell us so much. And, as we learn more about them we begin to know ourselves better. We have only to look and we will find the reflections of our own fears, love, hate and joy.

But we must look not with our eyes alone. As we look with love and compassion, as we "look" with all our senses to absorb the real meaning of those around us, we will perceive that they are we and we are they.

Thus we will discover the *Faces of Prayer*...within others and in ourselves.

Christopher Cross

Of all the things
God makes
a flower is the
most beautiful.
Look how they dance.
Oh, how I'd like to
dance like a flower.

Like Your trees
that grow together
so, now that
we are a family,
we too will
multiply and grow,
experience joy,
and rejoice
that we are together
in Your world.

Soon there will be
no more need for
my bigness.
Grant, Oh Lord, that
this feeling of wonder
never leaves me.

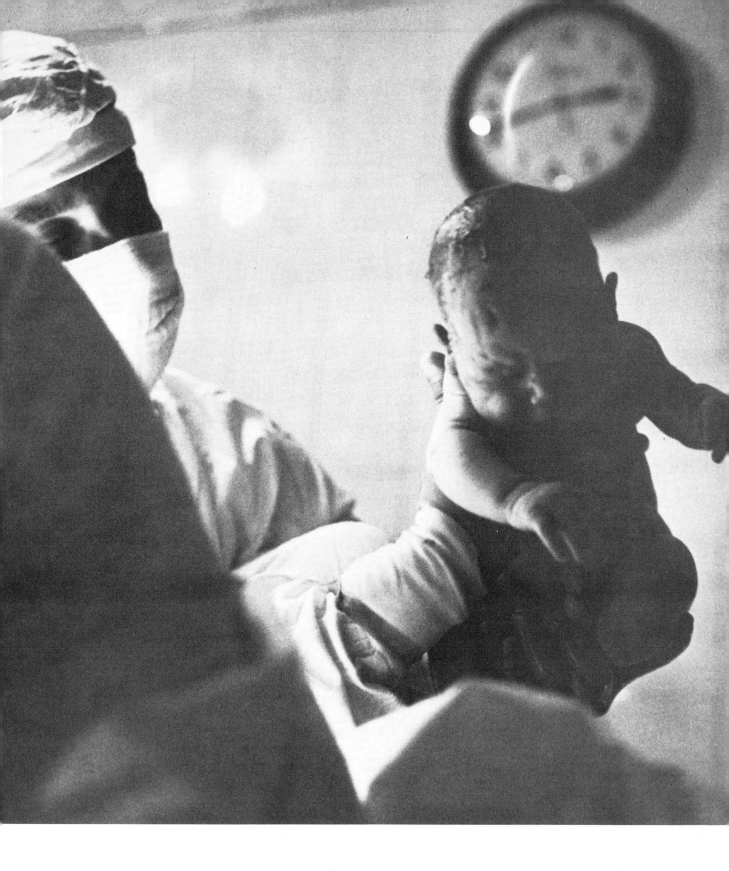

The time came... and she was born

*I looked at Your gift
and found the pain had
turned to joy*

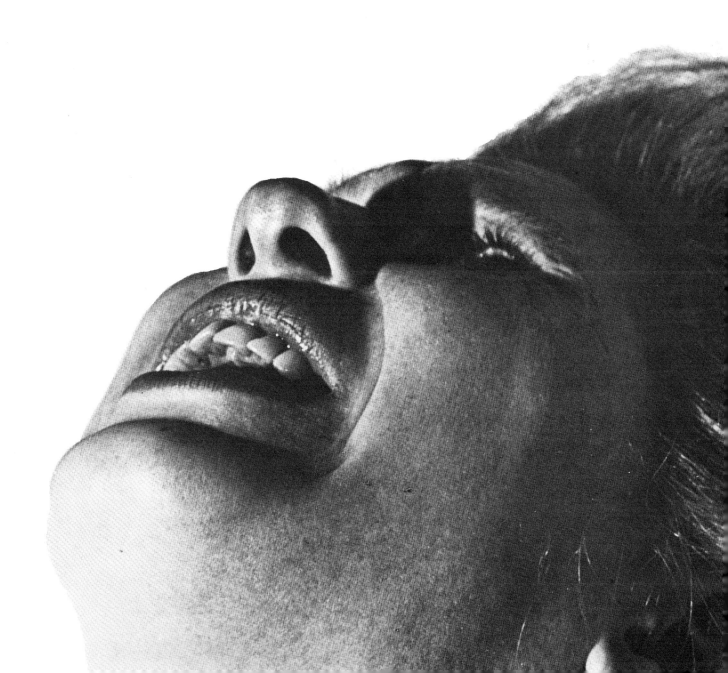

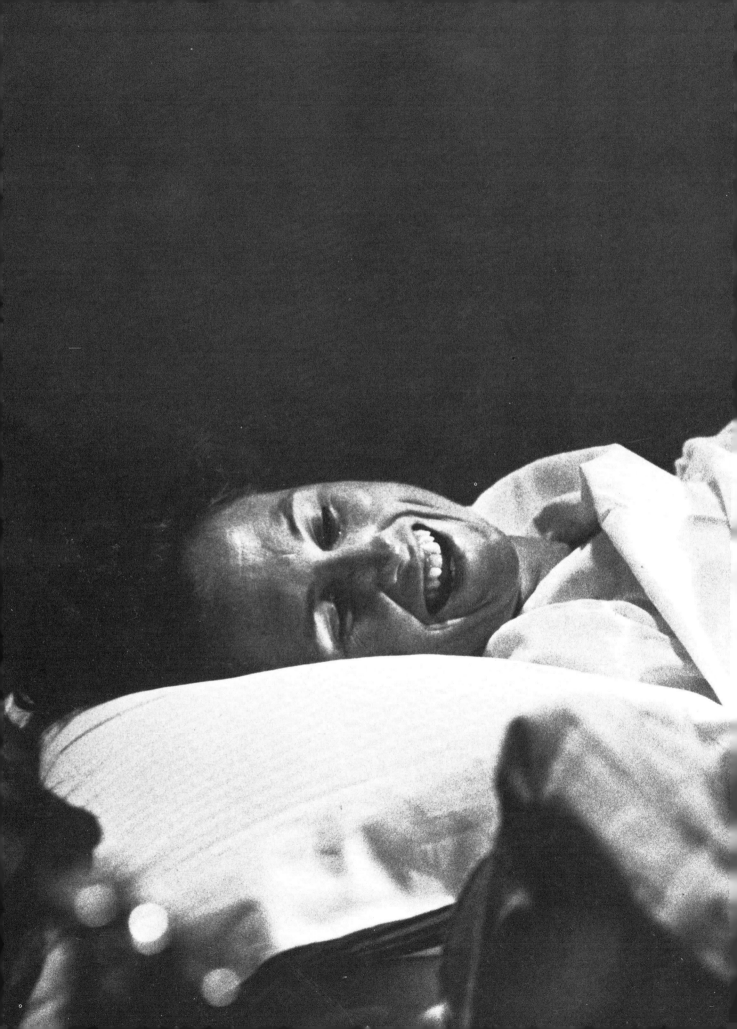

Miracle of miracles!
Thank You for the joy
and for Your help to
make her life a
reflection of Your
glory

Here, world,
is a precious new
bundle of pure people.
With Your blessings
they will remain pure
and fulfilled

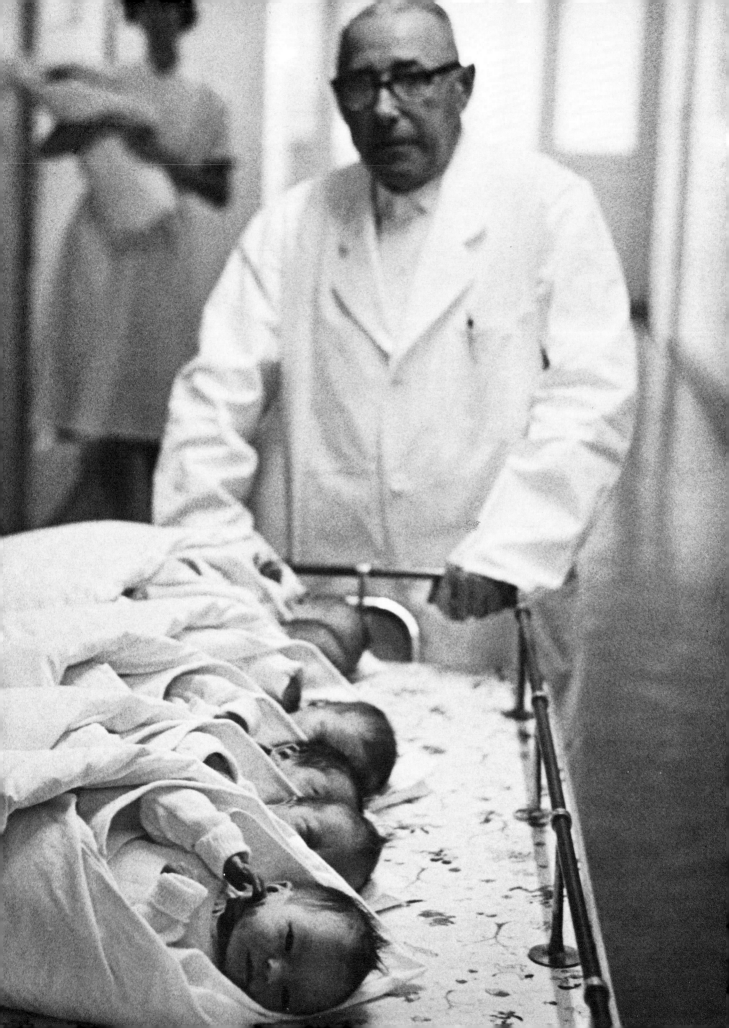

Help me to give him
the sustenance
of a life of
peace

Where are You anyhow?
Everytime we pray I look for You

For giving me Judy
who makes me feel God-like
I thank You

*Is God
like our daddy?
I hope so*

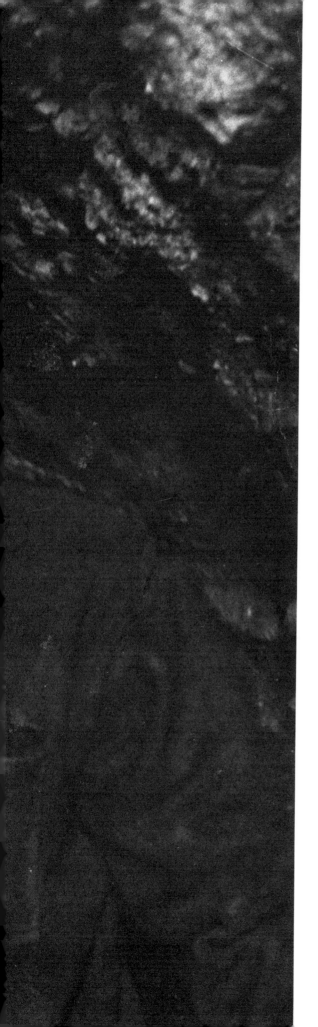

Between the digging
in the darkness
of Your earth
and the sleeping
in the darkness
of my nightmares—
don't get
to see Your sun
and stars.
When will they
shine on me...

How I pray
to be always
worthy of
His faith
and trust

Do You listen to prayers
of animals too?

*God grant that
what was good in my
life will make his life
even better*

Why do they
build the fences
so high and
so strong
against me?

How strong do we have to be, Jesus, to make it?

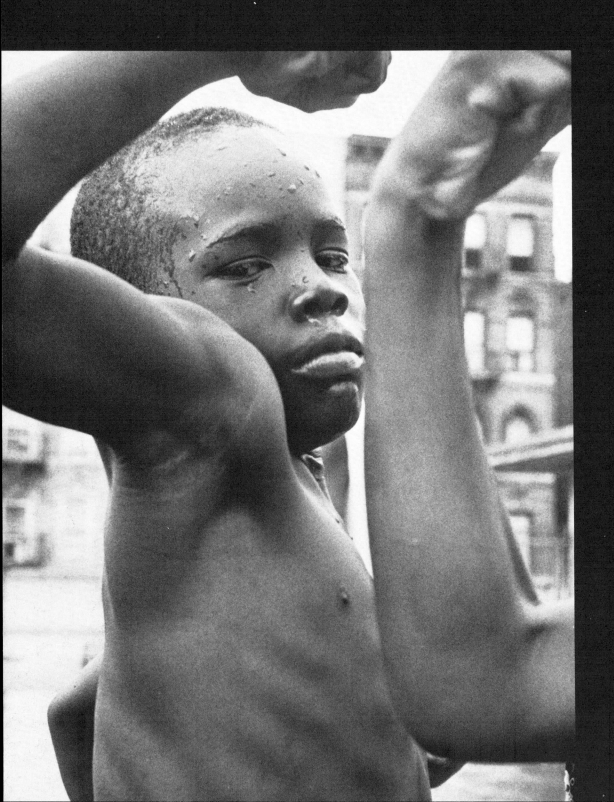

Thank you,
blessed Jesus
for making me strong
so I can bear the
pain of living

Whoever
You are—
wherever
You are—
who brought us
together...
Protect the
precious
harmony
of our
love

Blessed
Jesus—
How do I
explain this
to him?
I can't
tell him
this is
Thy will,
can I?

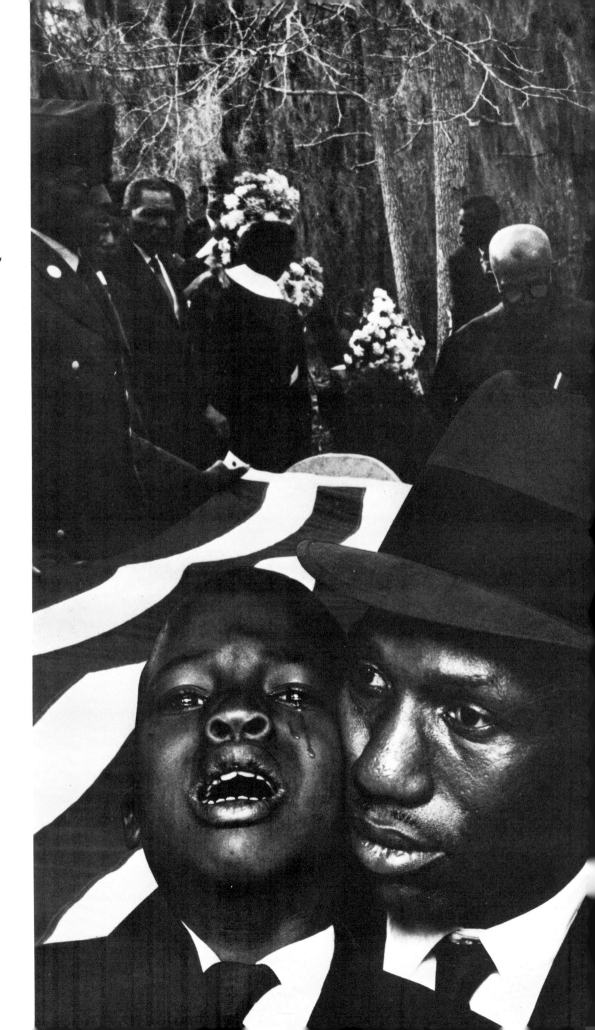

I struck out a lot.   Help him to connect.

When will we have our own place...
no longer to wander,
to be where You can find us?

I'm a
God-fearing
American —

*and America
is for real Americans…
and that's what I'm
teaching my boys in
Your name*

*Oh Lord,
we're taking
real good
care of
Your house
that gives
us comfort.*

We're doing it right Oh Lord ...making it Your heaven on earth now.

.D CRUSADE

NEW ORDER

*Ain't there
no God
for us?*

OFFICIAL SCENIC HISTORIC MARKER

CORONADO STATE
MONUMENT

← ½ Mile →

The ruins of the pueblo of Kuaua,
which was occupied when Coronado
...ored New Mexico, have been
...ated and partially restored,
...nusual feature of the pueblo
...painted kiva" which had been
...ted with several layers of
...lic murals. The museum
...houses pottery and other
...ound in the ruins.

Is Santa Claus really God?

It's been a lifetime of building for others...when, oh Lord, will they start building for us?

..You gave them
to me, then You
took them away.
Oh God, I'm so lonely.

Look what they're doing to Your children
all merciful One, all powerful One.
When will You stop it?

It's so
much fun
to be in
this world
of Yours

Tell us, Jesus...
will we ever have mommies and daddies too?

I can't see you God.....

My eyes
show me only
shadows—
so I'll try
real hard to
feel You.

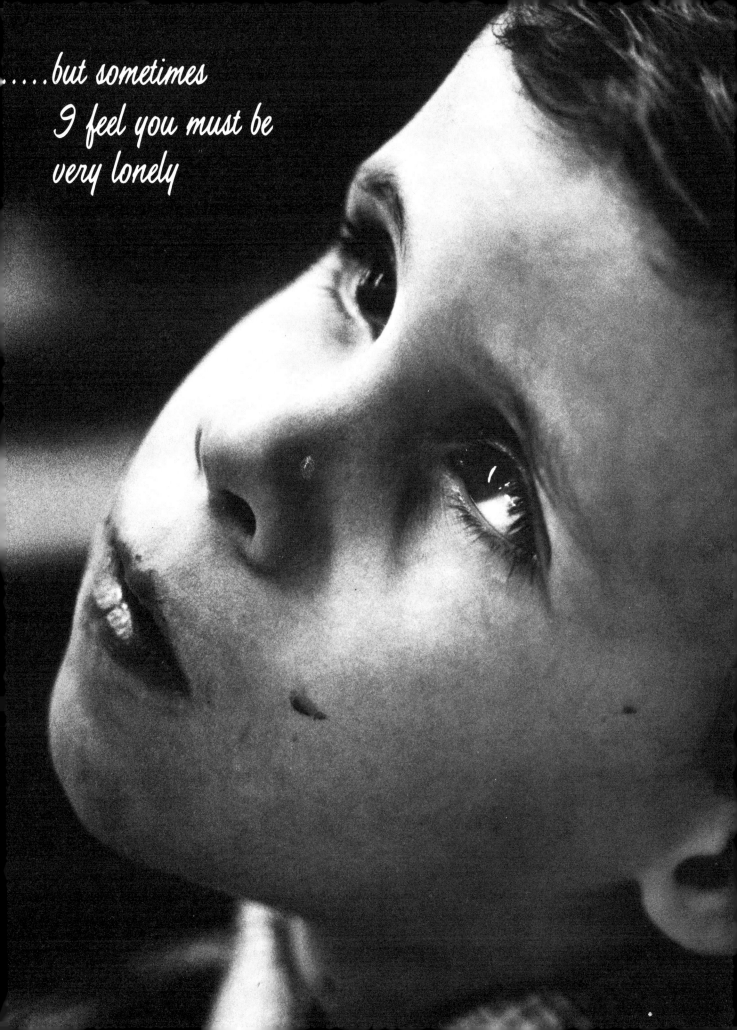

.....but sometimes
I feel you must be
very lonely

See him,
protect him,
give him
wisdom.
You will be
proud of
him.
I know
You will
dear God.

It's not lonely doing Your work
For I know You are at my side.

What shall I teach them?
What shall I show them?
How do I open their door
to Your truth, Your justice?

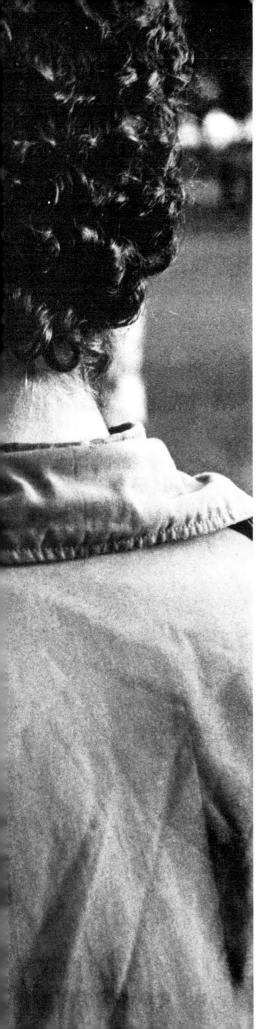

God, how we love.
Do You love us
so much too, God?

I did so little with this life of mine. He'll do more, dear God, with this precious life You've given him.

This's been my life...building with these tools, like You, Jesus, trying to build something good for people. I hope You like what I've done with my life...

Hear his little voice, Oh God
and help me to keep him
safe in Your world.

It's a hard life...
but they're all mine
and that makes it all
worthwhile. Thank You
for these precious gifts.

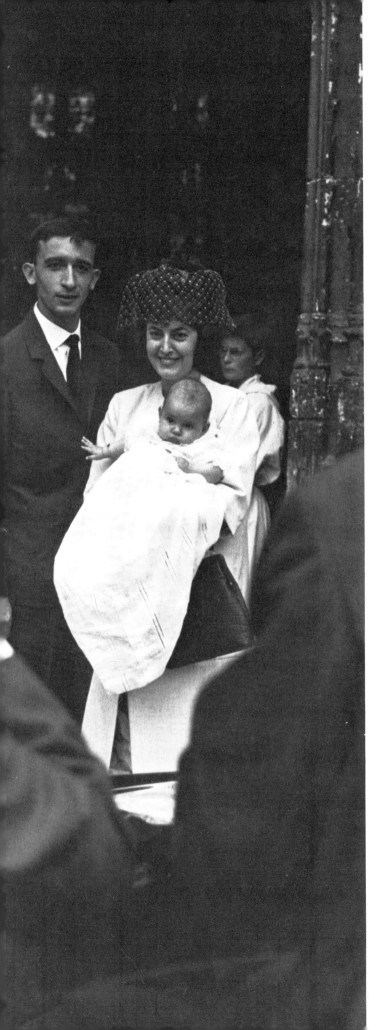

Here he is
dear God
baptized…
sanctified..
ready to take
his place
in Your world.

He's ready to become a man.
Help me, oh God, to be as ready to let him go.

*Will it be better
for me than it
was for them...*

*This is my family, Jesus... This is us.
Come meet us so I can thank You for all You've given.*

Please
God...

...no more killing.
Let him live
to use his learning
for himself,
for Israel

Sweet Jesus...I see You...I feel You...

You're in my heart...I know You're here

In all of God's world
there she was...
just for me.
Keep her near me
always

Thank You
for the life we've had.
Take us together,
dear Lord

This way, that way? Which way is Your way?

*I know
I don't
look so
good on
the outside.
But inside
I'm okay
So don't
be ashamed
of me
God.*

Must we forever be strangers in our own land?

Here, dear God, I am
closer to him.

Here is
where I'll be soon.

Take good care of him
until I join him.

Listen God
why do You keep my daddy in there
when I need him so much at home?

Help me to find the words,
the wisdom to bring them Your truth

You who are giver of life...
Protect her life—
don't take her away...

How I pray
that my hands
may embrace and
not restrain

How will You ever find me
behind all this steel and concrete...
just when I need You the most.

We're making music
for you.
Lord, are You listening?

Sometimes,
only
sometimes,
Jesus—
I think
You just
don't care
about us
black folk

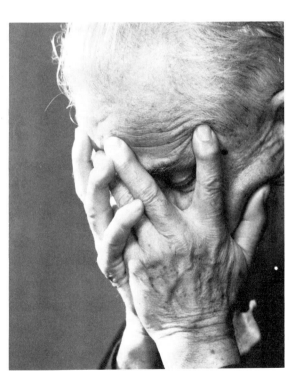

Where is the world You promised
me? Dear God I'm lost. Help me
find my way to You

*Together
we'll make it
to the end of
this road
and to the
beginning of
what's ahead.
For all of it
we thank You.*

Now we are one,
and for this
greatest gift
we thank You